What Are Literatur...

In *Literature Pockets—Caldecott Winners* the works o... come alive through fun, exciting projects. The activities ior eacn ot the 11 books, plus information about the Caldecott Medal, are stored in a labeled pocket made from construction paper. (See directions below.) Add the charming cover and fasten the pockets together. Your students now have their own Caldecott Medal Winners book to treasure.

How to Make the Pockets

1. Use a 12″ x 18″ (30.5 x 45.5 cm) piece of construction paper for each pocket. Fold up 6″ (15 cm) to make a 12″ (30.5 cm) square.

2. Staple the right side of the pocket closed.

3. Punch two or three holes in the left side of the pocket.

4. Glue the title strip onto the pocket. The title strip is found on the bookmark page for each book.

5. Store each completed project in the pocket for that book.

How to Make the Cover

1. Reproduce the cover decoration on page 3 for each student.

2. Students color and cut out the cover and glue it to a 12″ (30.5 cm) square piece of construction paper.

3. Punch two or three holes in the left side of the cover.

4. When all the pockets are completed, fasten the cover and the pockets together. You might use string, ribbon, twine, raffia, or metal rings.

Literature Pockets—Caldecott Winners • EMC 2701

How to Use Literature Pockets
Caldecott Winners

Basic Steps for Each Book

- State the name of the book, its author, and the award-winning illustrator.
- Read the book aloud to your students, showing the illustrations as you read.
- Show the illustrations again. Ask students to state their opinions about how the art adds to the enjoyment of the story. If appropriate, discuss the technique used to create the illustrations.
- Read and discuss the biographical information about the illustrator.
- Review the information on the bookmark about the illustrator. Then have students cut out the bookmark and glue it to a 5″ x 11 1/2″ (13 x 29.5 cm) piece of construction paper.
- Complete the writing activities and art experiences provided for each book.

Which Illustrations Are Best?

When all 11 books have been shared with the class, use the form on page 4 to vote for the class favorite. Continue voting until everyone agrees on one title, as is required by the Caldecott committee.

Other Caldecott Resources

- Collect other Caldecott Medal and Honor Book winners and set up a Caldecott library corner for students to enjoy.
- Check your library for books illustrated by Randolph Caldecott. *Ride a Cock-Horse and Other Rhymes and Stories* (Everyman's Library, 1995) is still in print.

Note: Reproduce this cover decoration for students to color, cut out, and glue to the cover of their Caldecott Winners book.

Name _____

Caldecott Award Winners

Name: _____

Mark the box in front of the book you think has the best illustrations.

☐ *Ox-Cart Man*

☐ *The Snowy Day*

☐ *Where the Wild Things Are*

☐ *Tuesday*

☐ *Joseph Had a Little Overcoat*

☐ *Always Room for One More*

☐ *Officer Buckle and Gloria*

☐ *Song and Dance Man*

☐ *Owl Moon*

☐ *Why Mosquitoes Buzz in People's Ears*

☐ *Arrow to the Sun: A Pueblo Indian Tale*

Caldecott Award Winners

Award Year	Title (Illustrator)
1938	*Animals of the Bible* (Dorothy Lathrop)
1939	*Mei Li* (Thomas Handforth)
1940	*Abraham Lincoln* (Ingri & Edgar Parin d'Aulaire)
1941	*They Were Strong and Good* (Robert Lawson)
1942	*Make Way For Ducklings* (Robert McCloskey)
1943	*Little House* (Virginia Lee Burton)
1944	*Many Moons* (Louis Slobodkin)
1945	*Prayer for a Child* (Elizabeth Orton Jones)
1946	*The Rooster Crows* (Maud & Miska Petersham)
1947	*The Little Island* (Leonard Weisgard)
1948	*White Snow, Bright Snow* (Roger Duvoisin)
1949	*The Big Snow* (Berta & Elmer Hader)
1950	*Song of the Swallows* (Leo Politi)
1951	*The Egg Tree* (Katherine Milhous)
1952	*Finders Keepers* (Nicolas Mordvinoff)
1953	*The Biggest Bear* (Lynd Ward)
1954	*Madeline's Rescue* (Ludwig Bemelmans)
1955	*Cinderella* (Marcia Brown)
1956	*Frog Went A-Courtin'* (Feodor Rojankovsky)
1957	*A Tree Is Nice* (Marc Simont)
1958	*Time of Wonder* (Robert McCloskey)
1959	*Chanticleer and the Fox* (Barbara Cooney)
1960	*Nine Days to Christmas* (Marie Hall Ets)
1961	*Baboushka and the Three Kings* (Nicolas Sidjakov)
1962	*Once a Mouse* (Marcia Brown)
1963	*The Snowy Day* (Ezra Jack Keats)
1964	*Where the Wild Things Are* (Maurice Sendak)
1965	*May I Bring a Friend?* (Beni Montresor)
1966	*Always Room for One More* (Nonny Hogrogian)
1967	*Sam, Bangs & Moonshine* (Evaline Ness)
1968	*Drummer Hoff* (Ed Emberley)
1969	*The Fool of the World and the Flying Ship* (Uri Shulevitz)

©2001 by Evan-Moor Corp.

Literature Pockets—Caldecott Winners • EMC 2701

1970	*Sylvester and the Magic Pebble* (William Steig)
1971	*A Story, A Story* (Gail E. Haley)
1972	*One Fine Day* (Nonny Hogrogian)
1973	*The Funny Little Woman* (Blair Lent)
1974	*Duffy and the Devil* (Margot Zemach)
1975	*Arrow to the Sun: A Pueblo Indian Tale* (Gerald McDermott)
1976	*Why Mosquitoes Buzz in People's Ears* (Leo & Diane Dillon)
1977	*Ashanti to Zulu: African Traditions* (Leo & Diane Dillon)
1978	*Noah's Ark* (Peter Spier)
1979	*The Girl Who Loved Wild Horses* (Paul Goble)
1980	*Ox-Cart Man* (Barbara Cooney)
1981	*Fables* (Arnold Lobel)
1982	*Jumanji* (Chris Van Allsburg)
1983	*Shadow* (Marcia Brown)
1984	*The Glorious Flight* (Alice & Martin Provensen)
1985	*Saint George and the Dragon* (Trina Schart Hyman)
1986	*The Polar Express* (Chris Van Allsburg)
1987	*Hey, Al* (Richard Egielski)
1988	*Owl Moon* (John Schoenherr)
1989	*Song and Dance Man* (Stephen Gammell)
1990	*Lon Po Po: A Red-Riding Hood Story from China* (Ed Young)
1991	*Black and White* (David Macaulay)
1992	*Tuesday* (David Wiesner)
1993	*Mirette on the High Wire* (Emily Arnold McCully)
1994	*Grandfather's Journey* (Allen Say)
1995	*Smoky Night* (David Diaz)
1996	*Officer Buckle and Gloria* (Peggy Rathmann)
1997	*Golem* (David Wisniewski)
1998	*Rapunzel* (Paul Zelinsky)
1999	*Snowflake Bentley* (Mary Azarian)
2000	*Joseph Had a Little Overcoat* (Simms Taback)
2001	*So You Want to Be President?* (David Small)

Caldecott Award Winners

The Caldecott Medal

**The Caldecott Medal—
A Minibook** .... pages 8 and 9
Provide two 6″ x 9″ (15 x 23 cm) pieces of colored construction paper for each student to use as a cover for their Caldecott Medal minibook. Read the book together to learn more about the award.

Randolph Caldecott .... page 10
Share this brief biography of the man for whom the Caldecott Medal was named. Read the biographical information to your students. Ask them to recall important details from Caldecott's life.

Pictures Help Tell the Story .... page 11
Students illustrate a nursery rhyme in their own style. Discuss how each illustrator adds to the meaning of the written word.

The Caldecott Medal

The Caldecott Medal is an award that is given by the Association for Library Service to Children, a part of the American Library Association. The medal is given each year to an illustrator of children's picture books. The winner's art must be in a book published in the United States.

At one time, books for children did not contain the interesting and colorful illustrations they do today. Randolph Caldecott was an illustrator in England in the 1800s. He drew the pictures for a series of children's books that were exciting to look at. The Caldecott Medal is named after him.

1

The Caldecott Medal honors the artists of children's books. It encourages artists to continue to produce excellent illustrations for children's books. The medal also keeps alive the memory of Randolph Caldecott.

A man named Frederic Melcher provided the first medal. It was awarded in 1938. His family has continued to provide the medal each year.

2

There are many wonderful picture books published every year. It is not always easy to decide which book should get the prize. The winner is chosen by a group of 15 people who are members of the American Library Association.

The members of the committee read each book and carefully study the pictures. They talk about the artwork. They ask each other questions about the books. They may even argue over choices. In the end, everyone must agree on only one book. However, the committee may choose books as "runners-up." These are called Honor Books.

3

Randolph Caldecott

Randolph Caldecott was born in England on March 22, 1846. He started to draw and model animals when he was only 6 years old. His father didn't want him to be an artist. This did not stop Randolph. He drew pictures everywhere he went.

When Randolph was 15 years old, he went to work in a bank, but still drew pictures. When he was 21, he went to the Manchester School of Art.

At first he sold drawings and cartoons to magazines and newspapers. He also drew pictures for books intended for adults. Later he created the illustrations for 16 picture books for children. Today Mr. Caldecott is best remembered for this series of picture books.

Mr. Caldecott drew in pen and ink on smooth paper. The drawings were photographed onto wood. Then engravers cut the wood to get it ready for printing. Different wood blocks were cut for each color that was needed for a picture.

Mr. Caldecott's health had never been very good. He moved to the United States in hopes that a warmer climate would improve his health. Unfortunately, in 1886, when he was only 39 years old, he died from heart disease. He is buried in the Evergreen Cemetery in St. Augustine, Florida.

Many people remembered how much they enjoyed reading Mr. Caldecott's books when they were children. In 1938 the Caldecott Award was created. Each year one illustrator would receive a medal. The medal was named after Randolph Caldecott because his drawings served as a model of what children's illustrations could be.

The Caldecott Medal

Pictures Help Tell the Story

Help students develop their own ideas about the value of beautiful, quality picture books in their own lives.

Preparation

Gather several picture books from the 1800s to the present. Use one of Randolph Caldecott's own books, if possible (*Ride a Cock-Horse and Other Rhymes and Stories* is still in print), an old reader such as a *McGuffey's Reader*, and a few Caldecott winners through the years. Include samples of black-and-white illustration, single-color illustration, and books with multicolor pages.

Materials

- sample books (see Preparation above)
- 9" x 12" (23 x 30.5 cm) art paper
- crayons, marking pens, colored pencils, paper scraps, watercolors, brushes
- several books of nursery rhymes

Steps to Follow

1. Share the illustrations in the books you collected. Discuss how picture books have changed over the years. Ask students to express their opinions about the illustrations shown—how they feel when looking at the illustrations; which illustrations make them want to read the book; how pictures help tell the story.

2. Have each student select a nursery rhyme to illustrate. They are to write the rhyme on their art paper and then illustrate it in an interesting or beautiful way. Remind them that the illustration should fit with the subject of the rhyme and that it should make the nursery rhyme more appealing to the readers. Allow students to choose the art media they wish to use.

3. Share the finished pictures. Compare the various styles used by different members in the class. Have students explain why they illustrated their verse in a particular way. Post the pictures on a bulletin board for all to share. When the pictures are removed from the board, place them in pocket 1 of students' Caldecott Winners books.

The Caldecott Medal

Barbara Cooney

Ox-Cart Man

About Barbara Cooney ....pages 14 and 15
Share the biography of Barbara Cooney and make her bookmark.

To Town and Back Home ....pages 16–19
Students create a flap book and recall what was taken to town and what was brought back.

Scratch a Picture ....page 20
Crayons, black paint, and a paper clip are all that students need to "scratch" out intriguing pictures.

All Year Long—A Flap Book ......pages 21–23
The farmer and his family worked all year long to make or collect things to sell in town. In this little flap book, students match pictures to show what goes together.

Barbara Cooney

"The pictures may be beautiful jewels in themselves, but they don't hang together unless there is a string of them, which is the text, and that's the foremost thing."

Barbara Cooney and her twin brother were born in a hotel room in Brooklyn, New York, on August 6, 1917. Her family lived in New York City, but she spent all of her childhood summers at her grandmother's house in Maine. As an adult she lived in Massachusetts where she and her husband raised four children. Later she moved to Maine where she lived near the sea.

Barbara was a self-taught artist. Her mother was a painter. She provided Barbara with all the art materials she wanted, but didn't give her lessons. Barbara did take a lot of art classes when she grew up, however.

Although she illustrated many books for other writers, Barbara didn't begin to write her own stories until after she had won her second Caldecott Medal.

Her first pictures were done in black and white. Later she began to use color. It was important to her that the details in her stories were correct. She traveled all over the world to do research. Some of her books didn't require that she go far. *Hattie and the Wild Waves*, *Miss Rumphius*, and *Island Boy* are stories based partly on her own life.

Barbara Cooney won the Caldecott Medal twice—for *Chanticleer and the Fox* and for *Ox-Cart Man*. She illustrated 110 books. Her last book, *Basket Moon*, was published in 1999. She died on March 10, 2000.

Barbara Cooney

"My favorite days were when I had a cold and could stay home from school and draw all day long."

Barbara Cooney

Won the Caldecott Medal for
- *Ox-Cart Man* (1980) by Donald Hall
- *Chanticleer and the Fox* (1959)

Other books by Barbara Cooney:
- *Miss Rumphius*
- *Island Boy*
- *Hattie and the Wild Waves*
- *Eleanor*

About Barbara Cooney
- She was born on August 6, 1917.

- She died on March 10, 2000.

- She was married to a doctor and had four children.

- She illustrated 110 books.

- She was such a kind person that when some mice made a nest in her car, she left them there. She just put rubber bands around her ankles to keep the mice from running up her pant legs while she was driving.

- She worked on her books in the room where her family liked to gather. She would often work late into the night after the rest of the family had gone to bed.

Caldecott 1980 Winner

Ox-Cart Man

Illustrated by Barbara Cooney • Written by Donald Hall

To Town and Back Home

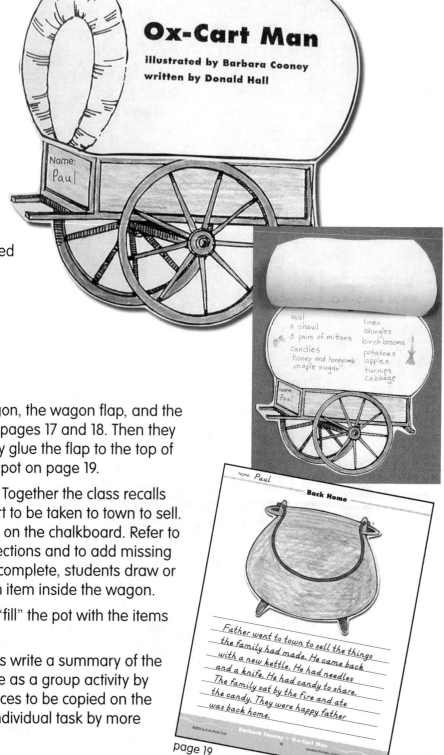

Students recall story elements as they "fill" the cart to go to market and the pot to bring back home. They then write a summary of the story.

Materials

- pages 17–19, reproduced for each student
- scissors
- glue
- crayons
- pencil

Steps to Follow

1. Students color the wagon, the wagon flap, and the top layer of the pot on pages 17 and 18. Then they cut out the pieces. They glue the flap to the top of the cart. They glue the pot on page 19.

2. Begin with the ox-cart. Together the class recalls the items put in the cart to be taken to town to sell. Write the items named on the chalkboard. Refer to the book to make corrections and to add missing items. When the list is complete, students draw or write the name of each item inside the wagon.

3. Repeat the process to "fill" the pot with the items to be taken home.

4. Using page 19, students write a summary of the story. This may be done as a group activity by your writing the sentences to be copied on the chalkboard, or as an individual task by more able students.

Barbara Cooney • Ox-Cart Man

glue

Name:

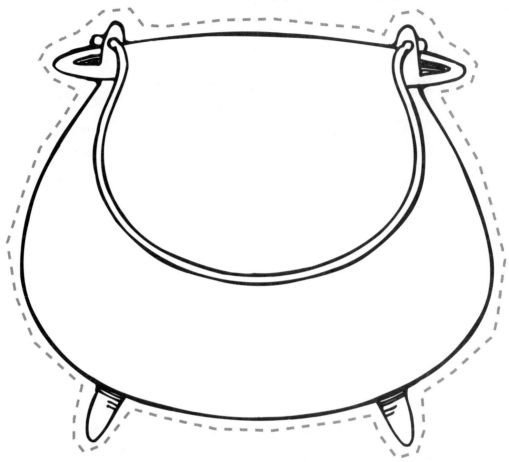

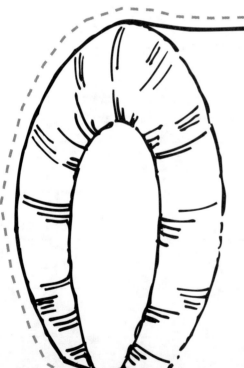

Ox-Cart Man

illustrated by Barbara Cooney
written by Donald Hall

18

Back Home

glue

_____

_____

_____

_____

_____

_____

_____

_____

19

Scratch a Picture

Barbara Cooney often used a technique called scratchboard to create illustrations. Share her Caldecott Medal story *Chanticleer and the Fox* as an example of this art form. Then have students scratch out pictures. Spread plenty of newspaper when the scratching starts, as this can be a bit messy.

Materials
- 6″ (15 cm) square white construction paper
- black tempera paint and paintbrush
- crayons
- paper clip
- newspaper
- paint smocks

Steps to Follow
1. Spread newspapers over worktables. Have students write their names on the back of their paper. Using crayons, cover the white paper with different-colored stripes of color. Use bright colors and color heavily over the entire paper.

2. Cover the entire paper with black tempera paint. Let it dry completely. (You may want to do the coloring and painting on one day, and then complete the lesson the next day.)

3. Unbend a paper clip. Use this to scratch off the paint to draw an animal, a scene, or a design. Encourage students to add details using hatch marks, curlicues, etc.

Barbara Cooney • Ox-Cart Man

 Literature Pockets—Caldecott Winners • EMC 2701

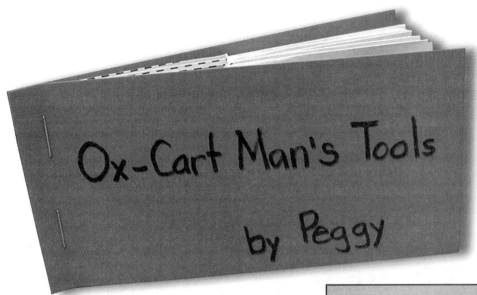

Recall how hard the family worked all year long producing items to sell in town. Then make this little flap book showing what was used to get the work done. Students match each picture to the tool used to make it or to the place it was gathered.

Materials

- page 22, three copies reproduced for each student
- page 23, one copy reproduced for each student
- scissors
- glue
- crayons
- two 2½″ x 5″ (6.5 x 13 cm) pieces of construction paper

Steps to Follow

1. Cut out the flap patterns (page 22) on the dotted lines. Fold on the fold line to make the flap. The folded flap should be on the right side of the page.

2. Color and cut out the pictures. Glue a tool or source on each folded flap.

3. Open up the flap and glue the item made or collected underneath.

4. Write a caption about the item on the writing lines. *(The hoe was used to dig in the garden.)* Students may use the remaining boxes to draw and write about other tools used in the story.

5. Stack the pages. Staple the construction paper cover to the left side.

6. Write a title on the cover.

Barbara Cooney • Ox-Cart Man

All Year Long

fold

paste

paste

fold

fold

paste

paste

fold

23

Ezra Jack Keats

The Snowy Day

About Ezra Jack Keats........ pages 25 and 26
Share the biography of Ezra Jack Keats and make his bookmark.

The Snowy Day .... page 27
Using a character from a magazine or newspaper, students write original stories about "The Snowy Day."

Snow Is… .... pages 28 and 29
Students print a shower of snowflakes, and then write a description of what snow is.

An Accordion Book .... pages 30 and 31
Students practice sequencing as they follow Peter's snowball as it melts in his pocket.

Ezra Jack Keats

"I'm an ex-kid. We all have within us the whole record of our childhood. What I do is address the child within myself. And try to be as honest as possible; then hope for the best."

Ezra Jack Keats was born in 1916 in Brooklyn, New York. His parents were immigrants from Poland. He began drawing when he was very young. His mother was proud of his artistic abilities, but his father didn't like his son to draw or paint. He felt his son would never be able to earn a living as an artist. This didn't stop Keats. He was determined to be an artist. It wasn't until his father died that Keats learned how proud his father had been of him. Keats found clippings in his father's wallet about all the prizes he had won.

Although Ezra Jack Keats won three college scholarships, he was unable to attend. He had to work to help support his family. Sometimes he only earned $1.00 a day.

He worked for a few years as an inker and illustrator for comic books, doing backgrounds for *Captain Marvel*. He also worked with the WPA, a government work program in the 1930s, as a mural painter. He took art classes at night whenever he could.

In 1954 he received his first job illustrating a children's book. Over the next ten years he illustrated 54 books. In the 1960s he began to write his own picture books for children. His stories began with pictures in his imagination. Then he would imagine the characters talking to each other.

Mr. Keats became the first American picture book maker to include children of all races as main characters in his books. He also wanted the children in his books to act like real children and do the things children really do.

Ezra Jack Keats illustrated more than 80 books for children. He died of a heart attack on May 6, 1983.

Literature Pockets—Caldecott Winners • EMC 2701

Ezra Jack Keats

> *"I taught myself to paint, using any kind of material I could find."*
>
> **Ezra Jack Keats**

Won the Caldecott Medal for
- *The Snowy Day* (1963)

Other books by Ezra Jack Keats:
- *Whistle for Willie*
- *Peter's Chair*
- *A Letter to Amy*
- *Goggles!* (Honor Book, 1970)
- *Hi, Cat!*
- *Apt. 3*
- *John Henry, An American Legend*

About Ezra Jack Keats
- He was born on March 11, 1916 and died on May 6, 1983.

- He began drawing when he was 4 years old.

- He sold a painting for 25 cents.

- He illustrated more than 80 books.

- Once, when he was a young boy, he covered the kitchen tabletop with drawings. He thought his mother would be mad, but she thought it was wonderful. She covered the table with a tablecloth. She uncovered it whenever they had company.

- He never saw a picture book when he was small. His family was too poor.

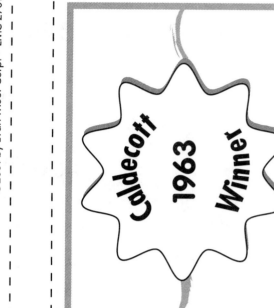

Caldecott
1963
Winner

The Snowy Day

Written and illustrated by Ezra Jack Keats

The Snowy Day

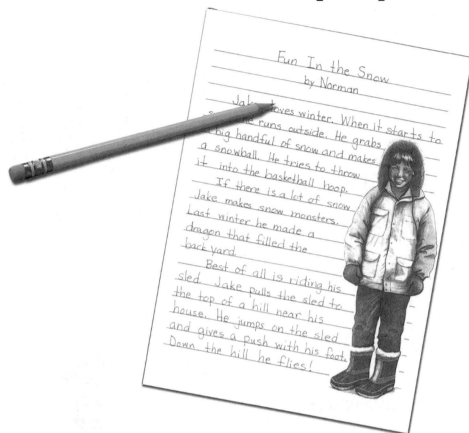

Fun In the Snow
by Norman

Jake loves winter. When it starts to snow he runs outside. He grabs a big handful of snow and makes a snowball. He tries to throw it into the basketball hoop.

If there is a lot of snow Jake makes snow monsters. Last winter he made a dragon that filled the back yard.

Best of all is riding his sled. Jake pulls the sled to the top of a hill near his house. He jumps on the sled and gives a push with his foot. Down the hill he flies!

Students write their own "Snowy Day" stories.

Materials

- writing paper
- pencil
- glue
- scissors
- an assortment of magazines and newspapers

Steps to Follow

1. Brainstorm a list of fun things to do in the snow. Include those in *The Snowy Day*, plus other fun activities. Write these on the chalkboard.

2. Explain to students that the little boy named Peter was inspired by a picture that Keats saw in *Life* magazine many years before he wrote *The Snowy Day*. (Peter was the main character in six other books by Keats.) Then ask students to find and cut out a picture of someone in a magazine or newspaper that they would like to write about.

3. Students glue the character to their writing paper. They pick two or three things from the "fun in the snow" list to use as they write a story about their character.

Students create a snowflake stamp from a foam meat tray. They print snowflakes and then write a description of snow.

Materials

- page 29, reproduced for each student
- 4″ (10 cm) square cut from a foam meat tray or florist foam
- sharpened pencil ("fat" primary pencil works best)
- blue tempera paint
- soft or foam paintbrush
- 4″ (10 cm) square white construction paper
- 6″ (15 cm) square blue construction paper
- glue
- scissors
- optional: spray glitter

Steps to Follow

1. Cut a corner section from a foam meat tray. You will need one piece per student.

2. Use the pencil to draw snowflakes on the piece of foam tray. Demonstrate how to press into the meat tray with the tip of a pencil without pushing all the way through it. Simple is best in designing snowflake shapes for the stamp.

3. Brush paint onto the stamp. Print the stamp onto the white paper. Optional: Spray the snowflakes with a little glitter for extra shine.

4. While the paint is drying, students write a description of snow on their snowflake forms.

5. Glue the snowflake picture to blue construction paper to create a frame. Cut out and glue the snowflake form to the reverse side of the paper.

Variation

Provide commercial snowflake stamps for students to use. Have them press the stamps into white paint and make a snowfall on midnight blue construction paper.

Ezra Jack Keats • The Snowy Day

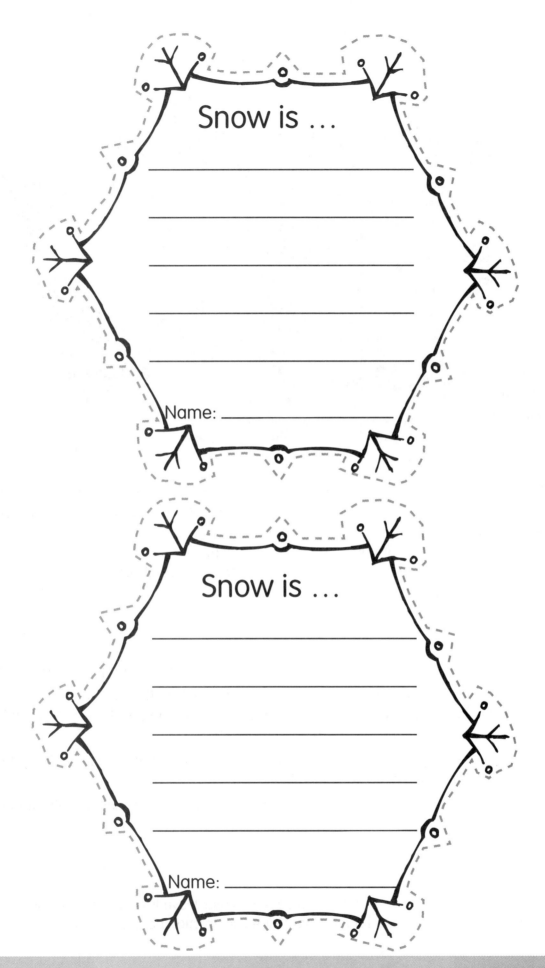

Snow is ...

_____

_____

_____

_____

Name: _____

Snow is ...

_____

_____

_____

_____

Name: _____

An Accordion Book

Students practice sequencing and writing descriptive sentences to show what happened to Peter's snowball.

Materials

- 6″ x 18″ (15 x 45.5 cm) red construction paper
- page 31, reproduced for each student
- scissors
- glue
- pencil

Steps to Follow

1. Fold the red paper as shown.

2. Cut apart the forms on page 31. Glue the title piece to the front.

3. Glue the story squares in order on the inside pages. Write a phrase or sentence describing what is happening in each picture.

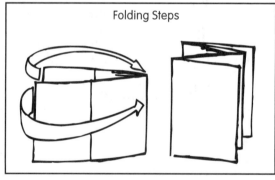

Folding Steps

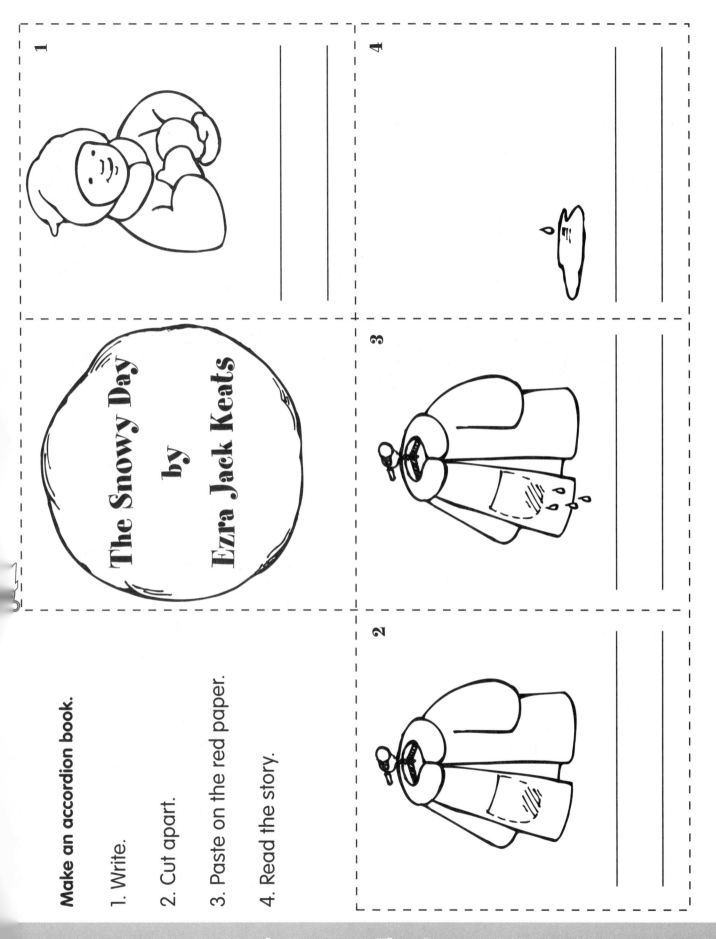

Make an accordion book.

1. Write.

2. Cut apart.

3. Paste on the red paper.

4. Read the story.

1

The Snowy Day
by
Ezra Jack Keats

4

3

2

Maurice Sendak

Where the Wild Things Are

About Maurice Sendak ...... pages 33 and 34
Share the biography of Maurice Sendak and make his bookmark.

What Could It Say? .... page 35
Wordless stories can set the imagination free. Share the wordless pages in *Where the Wild Things Are* with students and then invite them to draw their own text.

Wild Thing Puppets .... pages 36 and 37
Turn students loose to create fantastic "wild thing" stick puppets. Then take time for everyone to enjoy "creating a rumpus" with their puppets.

I Was Sent to My Room .... pages 38–40
Peek into students' bedrooms to see what sorts of "wild things" are creating a rumpus there.

Maurice Sendak

"The point of my books has always been to ask how children cope with a monumental problem...."

Maurice Sendak was born in Brooklyn, New York, in 1928. His parents were poor Polish immigrants. He was often sick as a child and had to stay in bed. His mother worried about him all of the time. His father read to him and told him stories before bedtime. His sister would bring him books from the library. As a young boy, his favorite illustrator was Randolph Caldecott, the man for whom the Caldecott Medal was named.

Maurice started working as an illustrator while he was still in high school. After finishing high school, he set up displays at a large toy store in New York City. He also took art classes at night.

Maurice published his first book when he was only 19 years old. Since then he has produced more than 80 books. Many of his stories have been inspired by Jewish tales he heard growing up. He still uses his childhood experiences in Brooklyn as ideas for his stories and drawings.

Mr. Sendak is a man of many talents. He wrote song lyrics for the animated film *Really Rosie.* He wrote the words for an opera based on *Where the Wild Things Are.* He has also designed sets and costumes for operas and worked on a ballet for children. He is always willing to try a new way to share his ideas and to create something wonderful for children.

Literature Pockets—Caldecott Winners • EMC 2701

Maurice Sendak

> "Although I'm getting old, my curiosity is strangely young, and I can't shut it up."
>
> Maurice Sendak

Won the Caldecott Medal for
- *Where the Wild Things Are* (1964)

He won the Caldecott Honor Medal for:
- *What Do You Say, Dear?* by Sesyle Joslin
- *The Moon Jumpers* by Janice May Udry
- *In the Night Kitchen*
- *Outside Over There*

About Maurice Sendak
- He was born on June 10, 1928, in New York.
- He has illustrated over 80 books.
- He named the main character of *In the Night Kitchen* after Mickey Mouse.
- At first *Where the Wild Things Are* was called "Where the Wild Horses Are." He couldn't draw horses very well so the title was changed.
- His mother worried about him when he was a boy. The moon in many of his books represents his mother looking out the window at him when he was a child.
- He has a German shepherd named Max.

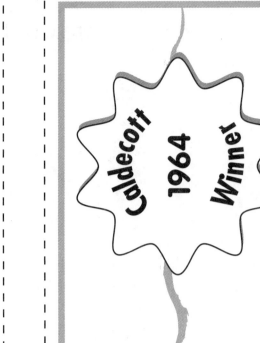

Caldecott 1964 Winner

Where the Wild Things Are

Written and illustrated by Maurice Sendak

What Could It Say?

After discussing Sendak's use of wordless pages in *Where the Wild Things Are*, students draw their own four-part wordless story.

Materials

- a copy of *Where the Wild Things Are*
- drawing paper
- pencils or crayons

Steps to Follow

1. Show the wordless pages one at a time. Ask students to describe what is happening in the picture. Explore how the pictures carry on the feeling of the story, showing rather than telling what is happening.

2. Students fold a sheet of drawing paper into fourths and then draw their own wordless story following these steps:

   a. Think about a character with a problem. Keep it simple (a lost dog, a birthday surprise, a flat tire on a bike, etc.).

   b. Plan what will happen to the character in each part of the story. Plan the solution to the character's problem before you start to draw.

   c. Draw each step of the story. Remember that the pictures must tell the whole story.

3. Provide time for students to share their wordless stories with classmates.

Wild Thing Puppets

Provide a bunch of "stuff" and turn your students loose to create wild and wonderful stick puppets.

Materials

- card stock cut into 9″ x 12″ (23 x 30.5 cm) pieces
- an assortment of paper in different colors, patterns, and textures
- feathers, glitter, buttons, raffia, etc.
- glue
- scissors
- crayons, colored pencils, marking pens
- paint stirrers, plastic straws, or thin doweling
- template on page 37, reproduced for each student

Steps to Follow

1. Look at the wild things in Sendak's book and discuss the features that make them "wild" looking. Discuss the types of things students can do to create a wild-looking creature.

2. Provide an accessible place for materials. Have students think about what they want their wild thing to look like. They then collect what they need from the supply area. (Set up behavior standards before students begin moving back and forth collecting materials.)

3. Students trace the template on page 37 onto the card stock and then cut it out to make the puppet's basic shape.

4. Add details to the puppet using marking pens, crayons, paper scraps, feathers, glitter, raffia, buttons, etc.

5. Glue the completed wild thing to a paint stirrer, plastic straw, or piece of doweling. After the glue is dry, provide time for students and their puppets to make a "rumpus."

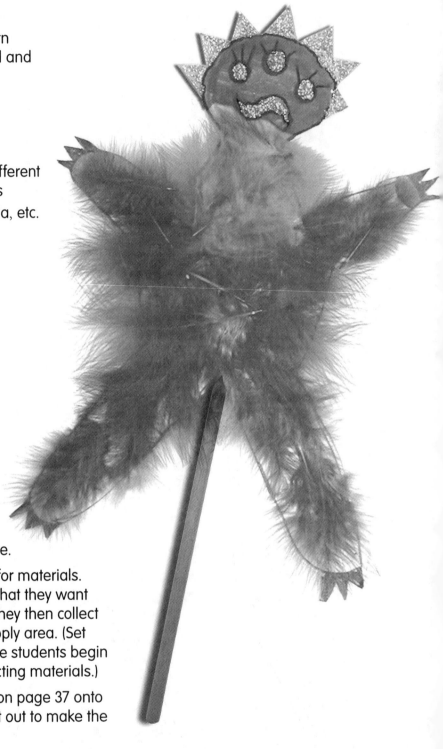

Maurice Sendak • Where the Wild Things Are

Basic Wild Thing Form

37

I Was Sent to My Room

Students make a folded paper book cover. They then complete a story using pages 39 and 40. Staple the completed story in the cover.

Materials
- 6″ x 8″ (15 x 20 cm) construction paper
- 5″ x 7″ (13 x 18 cm) construction paper
- scissors
- glue
- crayons
- pages 39 and 40, reproduced for each student

Steps to Follow

Make the bedroom door:
1. Draw a door on the 5″ x 7″ (13 x 18 cm) construction paper.

2. Fold a narrow flap along the left-hand side of the door. Glue the door to the 6″ x 8″ (15 x 20 cm) construction paper.

3. Open the door and draw "wild plants" growing in the bedroom. Encourage students to let some of the wild plants peek over the top and sides of the door.

4. After completing the story, staple the story pages in order under the bedroom door.

Write the story:
1. Recall what happened to the boy in the story. *(He misbehaved and was sent to his room without getting to eat his dinner.)* Ask students to think of things that might get them sent to their rooms.

2. Recall what he found in his room. *(It changed and wild things appeared. He had an imaginary adventure.)*

3. Explain that the story says that the boy and the wild things had a **rumpus**. Discuss what this means.

4. Go over pages 39 and 40 with students step by step. Have them fill in the blanks with their own ideas as you cover each part. They then add drawings.

5. Cut apart the sections and put them in order. Staple the story inside the bedroom door. Close the door over the story.

Maurice Sendak • Where the Wild Things Are

staple staple

WILD Things

by

____

I ______________________

____

____

so I was sent to my room.

In my room I saw a

____

_______________________,

a _____ ,

and a _____ .

We made a
noisy rumpus.

When Mother let
me come out of
my room,

_____

_____

_____

_____

_____

_____

_____ .

David Wiesner

Tuesday

About David Wiesner .... **pages 42 and 43**
Share the biography of David Wiesner and
make his bookmark.

Up, Up, and Away .... **pages 44 and 45**
What does the world look like when you are
floating up in the sky? Students use their
imaginations to create the world beneath
their floating frogs.

What Will I See Next? .... **page 46**
The last page of *Tuesday* shows the next
strange phenomenon to appear in the sky
(flying pigs). Discuss with students what other
strange animals or objects might fly or float by.

Share the picture at the time of 11:21. Explain
that this is a self-portrait of David Wiesner.
Have students draw portraits of themselves
looking out the window as though they are
seeing something unusual passing overhead
in the sky. What expressions might be on their
faces? Then students turn their papers over
and draw the unusual sight they imagined.

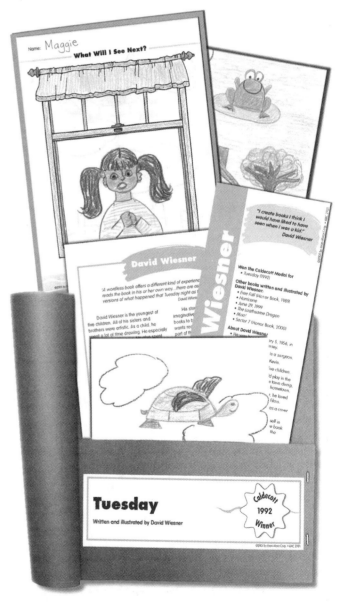

David Wiesner

"A wordless book offers a different kind of experience…Each viewer reads the book in his or her own way…there are as many versions of what happened that Tuesday night as there are readers."

David Wiesner (about his book Tuesday)

David Wiesner is the youngest of five children. All of his sisters and brothers were artistic. As a child, he spent a lot of time drawing. He especially liked to draw dinosaurs. He also spent hours studying the details in paintings by famous artists. He created his own comic book super-hero named Slop, the Wonder Pig.

David's first art training was a program on television where he learned about perspective, light, and scale. After high school he went to the Rhode Island School of Design. His favorite project there was to draw oranges that turned into ships and then into fish. He drew this on a piece of paper 10 feet (about 3 meters) tall. This painting inspired him to work on his first book *Free Fall*. If placed end to end, all the illustrations in *Free Fall*, except for the first and last pages, would be one long painting. It took him years to finish the book.

His stories and artwork are creative, imaginative, and funny. He wants his books to be fun and entertaining. He wants readers to "read" the pictures as part of the story.

David Wiesner and his wife, Kim, live in Brooklyn, New York, where he works on his illustrations and she works as a surgeon.

David Wiesner

> *"I create books I think I would have liked to have seen when I was a kid."*
>
> **David Wiesner**

Won the Caldecott Medal for
- *Tuesday* (1992)

Other books written and illustrated by David Wiesner:
- *Free Fall* (Honor Book, 1989)
- *Hurricane*
- *June 29, 1999*
- *The Loathsome Dragon*
- *Moo!*
- *Sector 7* (Honor Book, 2000)

About David Wiesner
- He was born February 5, 1956, in Bridgewater, New Jersey.
- His wife, Kim Kahng, is a surgeon.
- He has a son named Kevin.
- He is the youngest of five children.
- He and his friends would play in the cemetery, the woods, the town dump, and along the river of his hometown.
- When he was a teenager, he loved horror and science fiction films.
- His book *Tuesday* started as a cover for *Cricket* magazine.
- He painted a picture of himself in *Tuesday.* He is the man in the book who is eating a sandwich in the kitchen at 11:21.

Caldecott 1992 Winner

Tuesday

Written and illustrated by David Wiesner

The world looks very different when you are floating overhead. Students draw frogs floating on lily pads and then draw in the world below.

Materials

- page 45, reproduced for each student
  (or make an overhead transparency to show to the class as they draw)
- drawing paper
- crayons

Steps to Follow

1. Students follow the drawing steps to create a frog in the upper half of their drawing paper.

2. Share the pictures of the floating frogs in *Tuesday* again. Discuss what the world looks like from the frogs' perspective. What do things look like as the frogs float through the house? What do the buildings, cars, and plants look like as the frogs float through the sky?

3. Ask students to think about where the frogs they draw might be floating (over a house, above the trees, through their bedroom, across the school playground, etc.). Then they complete their pictures showing where their frogs are floating.

David Wiesner • Tuesday

Up, Up, and Away

Literature Pockets—Caldecott Winners • EMC 2701

Name:

Simms Taback

Joseph Had a Little Overcoat

About Simms Taback.......... pages 48 and 49
Share the biography of Simms Taback and make his bookmark.

An Old Saying................................. page 50
Simms Taback has filled this book with wonderful details. Share the endpapers of the book and the sayings on the walls. Then students write their own sayings and mount them in colorful collage frames.

What Did Joseph Make?............pages 51–53
This simple layer book helps students practice sequencing as they recall all of the ways Joseph reused the fabric in his old overcoat.

My Old Overcoat .... pages 54 and 55
After discussing the importance of recycling old items into a new form, students create a flap book to show one way to reuse their overcoats.

Simms Taback

"No artist is ever satisfied with his work, but usually we don't get to do it over."

Simms Taback (TAY-back) was born in the Bronx, New York. He grew up during the Depression. Although he and his neighbors were poor, he felt the Bronx was a special place to grow up in. There was a community center and a library. There also were science and sports clubs and art classes.

Simms went to a special high school for talented musicians and artists. He thought he would become an engineer, but his creative talents took over and he went on to study art at Cooper Union Art School.

Mr. Taback has been doing illustrations for over 40 years. He has made pictures for companies such as McDonalds and KFC, for television programs such as *Sesame Street,* for magazines and newspapers, and for a recording company. Today he is known for his posters, Smithsonian calendars, and greeting cards. He has also illustrated 35 children's books.

The Caldecott Medal-winning book, *Joseph Had a Little Overcoat,* began as a favorite Yiddish folk song from Mr. Taback's childhood. It is the second time he has illustrated the song. He used wonderful bright colors and funny details to bring the song to life. He set the story in a world he heard about as a child.

Simms Taback

> "I always knew I would end up being a children's book illustrator."
>
> **Simms Taback**

Won the Caldecott Medal for
- *Joseph Had a Little Overcoat* (2000)

Other books written and/or illustrated by Simms Taback:
- *The House That Jack Built*
- *There Was An Old Lady Who Swallowed a Fly* (Honor Book, 1998)
- *Too Much Noise* by Ann McGovern
- *Jason's Bus Ride* by Harriet Ziefert
- *When I First Came to This Land* by Harriet Ziefert

About Simms Taback
- He was born on February 13, 1932, in New York.
- He and his wife Gail live in Willow, New York.
- He has three grown children—Lisa, Jason, and Emily.
- He eats many chocolate bars with almonds, especially when he is working late at night.
- When his children were away from home, he would write, draw, or print postcards to send to them.

Caldecott 2000 Winner

Joseph Had a Little Overcoat

Written and illustrated by Simms Taback

After sharing the old sayings pinned to the walls in *Joseph Had a Little Overcoat*, students write their own sayings. Then they create fabric collages similar to the book's endpapers to frame them.

Materials
- 6″ x 9″ (15 x 23 cm) white construction paper
- 9″ x 12″ (23 x 30.5 cm) black construction paper
- scraps of colorful print fabric (precut into small geometric shapes for younger students)
- glue
- scissors

Steps to Follow
1. Write this pattern on the chalkboard:

   Better to _____ than _____ .

2. Ask students to think of different ways to end the saying. *(Better to eat your vegetables than to miss dessert. Better to clean your room than to have time out. Better to make a friend than to make an enemy. Better to wash your dirty hands than to get germs.)*

3. Students write their own saying on the white construction paper.

4. Glue the saying to the black construction paper.

5. Cut out and glue geometric fabric shapes (or use precut shapes) around the black edge to make a collage frame.

What Did Joseph Make?

After reading *Joseph Had a Little Overcoat*, list on the chalkboard the ways he used his old overcoat. Then students make this layer book.

Materials

- construction paper for book pages
  (pages may be all one color or assorted colors)
  - 4" x 9" (10 x 23 cm)   4" x 5" (10 x 13 cm)
  - 4" x 8" (10 x 20 cm)   4" x 4" (10 x 10 cm)
  - 4" x 7" (10 x 18 cm)   4" x 3" (10 x 7.5 cm)
  - 4" x 6" (10 x 15 cm)   4" x 2" (10 x 5 cm)
- patterns on pages 52 and 53, reproduced for each student
- crayons, marking pens, or colored pencils
- scissors
- glue
- stapler

Steps to Follow

1. Lay the longest piece of paper on the desk. Place the remaining pieces in order, starting with the smallest piece and ending with the 4" x 8" (10 x 20 cm) piece on top.

2. Staple along the top edge through all pages. (An adult may need to do this.)

3. Cut out all of the pictures of Joseph's clothing. Glue the overcoat on the first page as shown. Then write "overcoat" on the part of the bottom sheet that shows under the top sheet.

4. Lift the flap and glue the jacket on the next flap. Write "jacket" on the back layer above "overcoat." Continue pasting pictures and writing until all the items are in the book.

Joseph had a little...

53   Literature Pockets—Caldecott Winners • EMC 2701

The illustrated page shows:

©2001 by Evan-Moor Corp.

I had an overcoat.

So I made a vest.

Name Raul S.

55

Literature Pockets—Caldecott Winners • EMC 2701

Students illustrate one way to use an old overcoat.

Materials

- page 55, reproduced for each student
- scissors
- crayons
- glue

Steps to Follow

1. Students draw themselves wearing the overcoat on the activity page.

2. Students color a plaid pattern on the coat with their crayons.

3. Students carefully cut along the cut lines on the page.

4. Students fold along the fold lines. Cut out the vest shape on the folded portion.

5. Students draw in the rest of the body around the vest.

6. Students glue the "So I made a vest" box under the vest on the front of the folded portion.

Simms Taback • Joseph Had a Little Overcoat

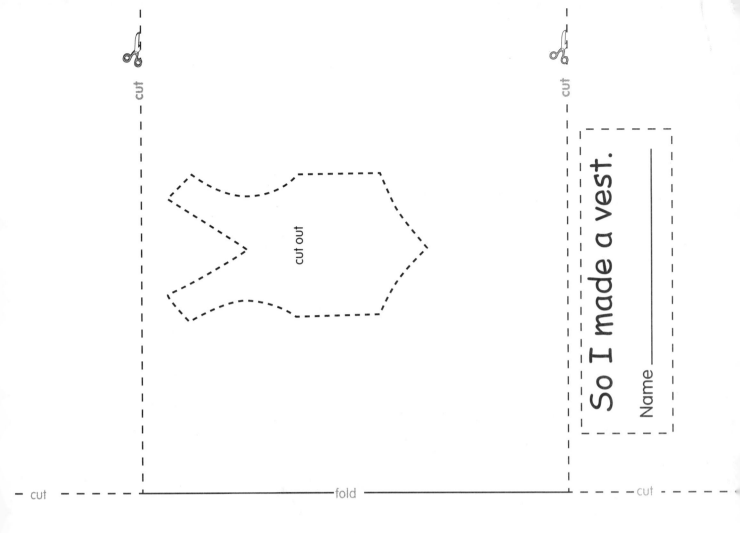

cut out

So I made a vest.

Name _____

cut — — — fold — — — cut

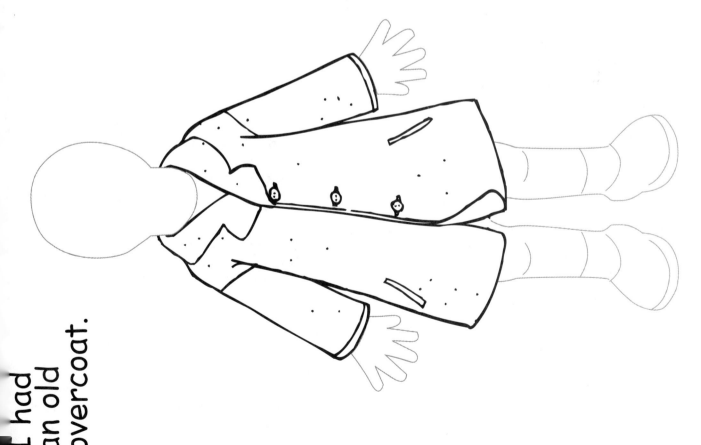

I had
an old
overcoat.

55

Nonny Hogrogian

Always Room for One More

About Nonny Hogrogian .... pages 57 and 58
Share the biography of Nonny Hogrogian and make her bookmark.

Wee House in the Heather .... page 59
Students use black crosshatching and a bit of sponge painting to capture the feeling of the art in this story.

Scottish Dictionary .... page 60
Poof! It's a book. Students cut and fold this page to make a tiny eight-page dictionary of Scottish words. Then, using lined paper, they write a sentence using each word to show what it means.

Always Room for One More .... pages 61 and 62
Lachie MacLachlin's house was always full. Students pull a tab to fill their houses with a series of visitors.

Nonny Hogrogian

"I am always dissatisfied with my work, always left with the feeling that I must try harder next time...."

Nonny Hogrogian (NON-ee ho-GROW-gee-un) came from a family of artists. Her mother, father, grandfather, and an aunt were all artists. When she was a child, she would look through books and dream of making beautiful pictures of her own.

In high school Nonny created handmade cards for her friends and family. She made scratchboard pictures for the school magazine. After high school she went to college in New York where she studied art. From there she went to work for a publisher where she supervised the creation of book jackets. Sometimes she got to do the artwork herself.

Nonny Hogrogian is of Armenian heritage. She likes to tell folktales from her family's culture. She does a lot of research about the dress, features, and customs of the people she draws. She studied the people and villages of Scotland before doing the pictures for her award-winning book *Always Room for One More*.

She and her husband, David Kherdian, have worked together on many books.

Nonny Hogrogian

> *"When I was about three or four years old, I began to putter with my father's paints and brushes."*
> Nonny Hogrogian

Won the Caldecott Medal for
- *Always Room for One More* by Sorche Nic Leodhas (1966)
- *One Fine Day* (1972)

Other books written and/or illustrated by Nonny Hogrogian:
- *The Cat Who Loved to Sing*
- *The Contest* (Honor Book, 1977)
- *The Glass Mountain*
- *The Dog Writes on the Window with His Nose and Other Poems* by David Kherdian

About Nonny Hogrogian
- She was born on May 7, 1932, in New York.
- She is married to David Kherdian.
- She likes to tell folktales from her family's Armenian heritage.
- She likes music by Vivaldi and Bach.

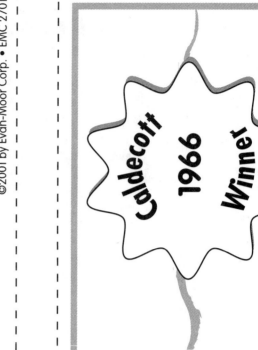

Caldecott 1966 Winner

Always Room for One More

Illustrated by Nonny Hogrogian • Written by Sorche Nic Leodhas

Wee House in the Heather

Students create their own wee house sitting in a field of sponge-painted heather. Share the cover illustration to remind students of how the wee house had been drawn in black and how crosshatch marks were used to fill in the spaces. Then note how the heather on the hill is done with splotches of pink and green.

Materials
- 4½" x 6" (11.5 x 15 cm) white construction paper
- small pieces of sponge
- paper plates
- tempera paint—gray, pink, green
- pencil or black drawing pencil

Steps to Follow
1. Create the hillside by painting with sponges across the bottom of the page. Use gray for the ground and pink and green for the heather plants.

2. Sponge a gray cloud in the sky. Let the paint dry.

3. Draw a small house with a pencil. Complete the house using crosshatch marks. Encourage students to add details such as smoke coming out of a chimney or birds flying in the sky.

Note: Reproduce this page to use with "Scottish Dictionary" on page 56.

cut

wee
little

A wee mouse peeked out of its hole.

8.

fold 1

porridge
cooked cereal

"Come eat your porridge."

7.

fold 3

Scottish Dictionary

_____'s

Och (awk)
Oh

"Och! I hurt my knee," he cried.

6.

fold 2

fold 2

bairns
young children

Two bairns sat on the grass.

2.

canny
clever, wise

She was a canny old woman.

5.

fold 3

blether
foolish talk

"I don't want to hear such blether," said the teacher.

3.

fold 1

brae (bray)
grassy hill

Sheep were grazing on the green brae.

4.

cut

Nonny Hogrogian • Always Room for One More

Literature Pockets—Caldecott Winners • EMC 2701

Lachie MacLachlin's house always had room for one more visitor during the storm. Students draw visitors who might come to fill up their homes on a stormy day. These visitors may be real or imaginary.

Materials

- page 62, reproduced for each student
- 3″ x 18″ (7.5 x 45.5 cm) white construction paper
- crayons
- scissors
- glue

Steps to Follow

1. Recall all who came to Lachie MacLachlin's house. (Refer to the book to jog memories.) Ask students to think about who might come to their door on a stormy day. List their ideas on the chalkboard (mail carrier, aunts, uncles, cousins, a big wet dog, etc.).

2. Color and cut out the house. Cut slits. (An adult will need to do this for younger students.)

3. Draw people in the house.

   a. Slip the paper strip into the house.

   b. In the window, draw the people (and animals if you like) that already live in your house.

   c. Pull the strip to the left until the window is empty. Draw a "stormy weather" visitor in the window.

   d. Continue pulling the strip and drawing visitors until there is no more room on the strip.

4. Tape the house together above and below the pull strip.

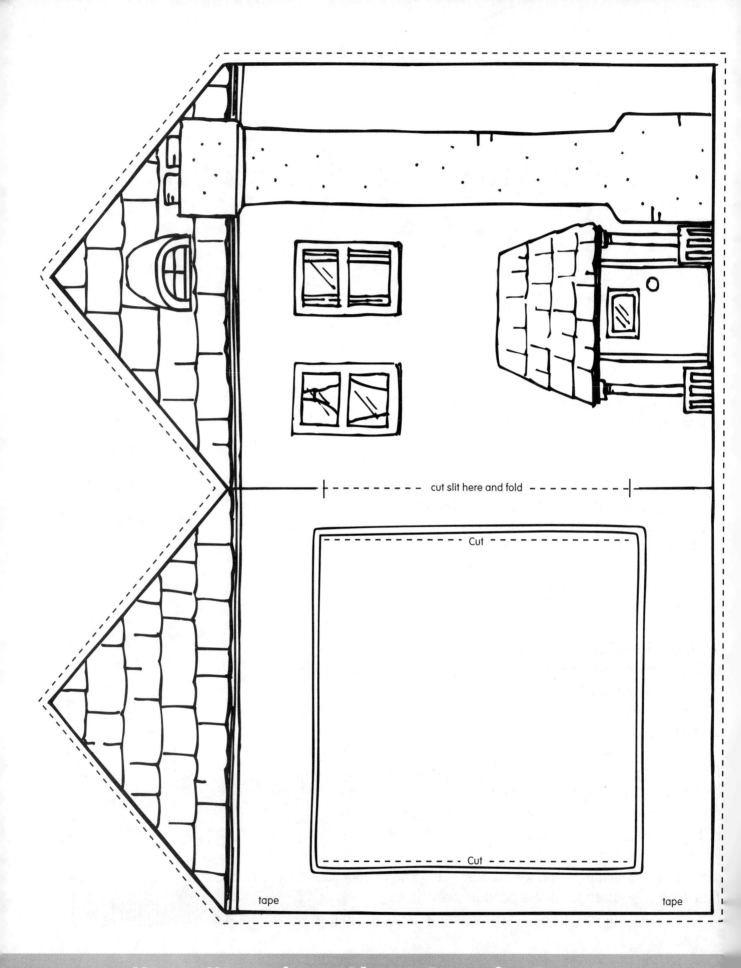

cut slit here and fold

Cut

Cut

tape   tape

Peggy Rathmann

Officer Buckle and Gloria

About Peggy Rathmann...... pages 64 and 65
Share the biography of Peggy Rathmann and make her bookmark.

Safety Tip Stars................................. page 66
Share the stars on the endpapers of the book that contain safety tips. Ask students to think of other tips for living safely. Students then write and illustrate one tip of their own. Post these on a bulletin board. Later, place the stars into students' Officer Buckle and Gloria pockets.

Working Together .... page 67
Officer Buckle and Gloria did their best work when they worked together. Using page 67, students write about a time when they worked with someone to get a job done.

Draw a Dog .... page 68
Using a permanent black marking pen, students follow the steps on page 68 to draw a dog. They paint the dog with watercolors. While the painting dries, students write a paragraph describing what is special about this dog. They then tape the paragraph to the back of their paintings.

Peggy Rathmann

"There's a funny thing that happens between words and pictures. A picture book is a special medium. Because the pictures don't work without the words and the words don't work without the pictures. Pictures enable me to make a better story than I could with words alone."

Margaret Crosby Rathmann was born and raised in Minnesota. She had a happy childhood playing with her two brothers and two sisters in the backyard. They built snow creatures in the winter and played in a plastic wading pool in the summer.

After high school she went to several colleges, finally graduating from the University of Minnesota. She studied art and writing at the University of Minnesota and the Otis School of Design in Los Angeles, California.

She started to write stories to entertain her young nieces. Her stories are often based on her own life. Her first book, *Ruby the Copycat*, was a prizewinner. It was based on her feelings that her own ideas were not good enough, so she copied her classmates' stories. The idea for *Good Night, Gorilla* came from a childhood memory. It took her two years and ten different endings to finish the book.

Officer Buckle and Gloria, her Caldecott Medal winner, was inspired by a family video in which the family dog licked all the poached eggs without anyone noticing what was going on. It was only later while watching the video that they saw what the dog had done. By then the eggs had already been eaten! *Officer Buckle and Gloria* is a story that could not be understood by only reading the words. The words and pictures work together to get the plot across.

Peggy Rathmann lives in San Francisco with her husband, John Wick. She travels around the country reading from her picture books and doing drawing demonstrations for children.

Peggy Rathmann

> *"...since then all of my books have been based on embarrassing secrets."*
> **Peggy Rathmann**
> *(after Ruby the Copycat)*

Won the Caldecott Medal for
- *Officer Buckle and Gloria* (1996)

Other books by Peggy Rathmann:
- *Ruby the Copycat*
- *Good Night, Gorilla*
- *Bootsie Barker Bites*
- *10 Minutes Till Bedtime*

About Peggy Rathmann
- She was born on March 4, 1953, in Saint Paul, Minnesota.
- She is married to John Wick and lives in San Francisco, California.
- She wanted to teach sign language to gorillas. After a class in signing, she decided she would rather draw pictures of gorillas.
- When she was in school, she made campaign posters for her brother. They were so beautiful that other students took the posters home.
- She gets her ideas for books from her own life.
- In *Bootsie Barker Bites*, she made Bootsie look like herself so she wouldn't offend anyone else.

Caldecott 1996 Winner

Officer Buckle and Gloria

Written and illustrated by Peggy Rathmann

Note: Reproduce this page to use with "Safety Tip Stars" on page 63.

1. Cut out the star.
2. Write a safety tip on the star.
3. Draw a picture showing the safety tip.

Name

Safety Tip

Working Together

_____	_____
name	name

and

Draw a Dog

How to Draw a Dog

1.

2.

3.

4.

Stephen Gammell

Song and Dance Man

About Stephen Gammell..... pages 70 and 71
Share the biography of Stephen Gammell and make his bookmark.

Dancing Man .... pages 72 and 73
Students make a stick puppet that can "dance."

Then and Now .... page 74
Using the form on page 74, students interview their own grandfather (or other older family member, friend, or neighbor) to find out what that person did as a young man and what he does now.

Students use the information they gathered to write a story about the person interviewed.

Stephen Gammell

"My first concern is to serve the story. That is an illustrator's job."

Stephen Gammell was born in Iowa. As a young boy, he liked to draw soldiers, airplanes, trains, and cowboys and Indians. He didn't think about earning his living as an artist when he grew up. His father would help him draw and supplied him with paper and pencils. His father never coached Stephen or told him how to work.

For several years after college, Stephen worked doing odd art jobs for local stores and magazines. He started illustrating books when a publisher saw samples of his work and asked him to draw the pictures for a book. He has worked as an illustrator ever since.

Mr. Gammell likes history and music. He likes to go camping, backpacking, canoeing, bicycling, and traveling. He still likes to draw pictures of Western history.

He goes to work in his second-floor studio every day. He says he is happy to work alone. He likes to work on one book at a time and likes to do the whole book design. His work is warm, playful, and full of energy.

Stephen Gammell

> *"I love my work. I love drawing, painting, and making books."*
> **Stephen Gammell**

Won the Caldecott Medal for
- *Song and Dance Man* by Karen Ackerman (1989)

Other books written and/or illustrated by Stephen Gammell:
- *Once Upon MacDonald's Farm*
- *Where the Buffaloes Begin* by Olaf Baker (Honor Book, 1982)
- *The Relatives Came* by Cynthia Rylant (Honor Book, 1986)
- *Old Black Fly* by Jim Aylesworth

About Stephen Gammell
- He was born on February 10, 1943, in Iowa.
- His father was an art editor for a magazine publisher.
- He has written only four of his own books because he finds writing very difficult and would rather illustrate someone else's text.
- He used to cut up magazines to make scrapbooks.
- He plays the guitar, banjo, mandolin, and piano.

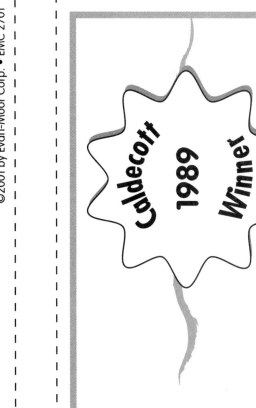

Caldecott 1989 Winner

Song and Dance Man

Illustrated by Stephen Gammell • Written by Karen Ackerman

Dancing Man

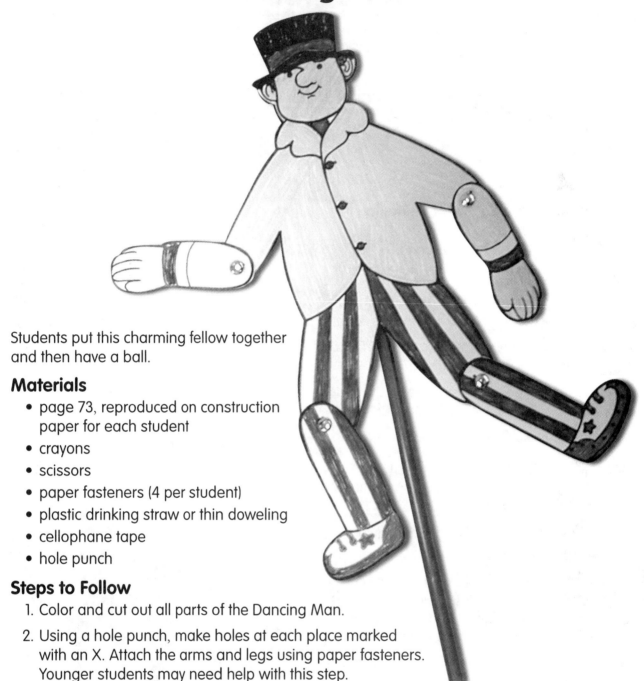

Students put this charming fellow together and then have a ball.

Materials

- page 73, reproduced on construction paper for each student
- crayons
- scissors
- paper fasteners (4 per student)
- plastic drinking straw or thin doweling
- cellophane tape
- hole punch

Steps to Follow

1. Color and cut out all parts of the Dancing Man.

2. Using a hole punch, make holes at each place marked with an X. Attach the arms and legs using paper fasteners. Younger students may need help with this step.

3. Tape the straw or doweling to the back of the Dancing Man. Jiggle it to make him "dance."

Dancing Man

73

Name: _____

Then and Now

┌─────────────────────────────────────┐
│   │
│   │
└─────────────────────────────────────┘
person being interviewed

picture or photograph

picture or photograph

What I did when I was [ ] years old.   What I do, now that I am [ ] years old.

• _____   • _____

_____   _____

_____   _____

• _____   • _____

_____   _____

_____   _____

• _____   • _____

_____   _____

_____   _____

Stephen Gammell • Song and Dance Man

John Schoenherr

Owl Moon

About John Schoenherr ...... pages 76 and 77
Share the biography of John Schoenherr and make his bookmark.

A Moonlit Night .... page 78
Students create black trees in the snow against a moonlit sky. They then add an interesting simile about the trees.

Draw an Owl .... page 79
Students follow the drawing steps to create a wonderful owl, adding details with crayons or marking pens. They then mount the finished drawings on midnight blue construction paper.

If You Go Owling .... pages 80 and 81
Recall the guidelines for a successful owling outing. Then students complete the form on page 81 to create "owling" charts.

John Schoenherr

"Whether I'm painting a stone or a barrel or a bear, I want to make it exist."

John Schoenherr (SHOW-en-her) was born in New York City. His mother came from Hungary and his father came from Germany. He spoke German as a child. He used drawing to communicate with the children in his neighborhood who spoke many other languages.

John started art lessons when he was 13 years old. Today he creates paintings to exhibit, covers for science fiction books, and pictures for children's books.

It is a little unusual for a wildlife artist to have been born and raised in New York City. Mr. Schoenherr developed a love of nature and animals by visiting natural history museums and zoos. After moving his family to the country in New Jersey, he started to draw more wildlife and nature pictures. Most of his children's books are about animals or nature.

Instead of using a lot of details, Mr. Schoenherr likes to use strong colors and shapes to develop a picture.

John Schoenherr • Owl Moon

John Schoenherr

"I think I identify with wild animals, sometimes even more than with people. A friend of mine likes to say that I'm a bear disguised as a human being."
John Schoenherr

Won the Caldecott Medal for
- *Owl Moon* by Jane Yolen (1988)

Other books written and/or illustrated by John Schoenherr:
- *The Barn*
- *Bear*
- *Rascal* by Sterling North
- *Gentle Ben* by Walter Morey
- *Julie of the Wolves* by J. C. George

About John Schoenherr
- He was born on July 5, 1935, in New York City.
- He has a wife, Judith, and two children, Ian and Jennifer.
- He received his first watercolor set when he was 8 years old.
- He has illustrated the covers of more than 300 science fiction books.
- He learned English by reading comic strips.
- He likes to explore caves and climb rocks.

Caldecott 1988 Winner

Owl Moon

Illustrated by John Schoenherr • Written by Jane Yolen

A Moonlit Night

The tree stood as still as a rabbit frightened by a fox.

Students create dark trees and glimmering snow against the night sky.

Materials

- 9″ x 12″ (23 x 30.5 cm) white construction paper
- watercolors (dark blue, very light blue)
- watercolor brushes
- black tempera
- plastic straws
- 3″ (7.5 cm) square of white paper
- writing paper
- scissors
- glue

Steps to Follow

1. Across the top 2/3 of the page, paint the night sky using dark blue watercolor.

2. Across the bottom 1/3 of the page, paint very light blue (almost clear) watercolor for snow. Allow the paint to dry.

3. Drop black tempera on the paper in the middle of the snow. Blow through a straw to move the paint to form the tree. (If this is a new technique for your students, practice on scrap paper before beginning the final picture.)

4. Round the corners of the white paper square to make a moon. Glue it in the sky.

5. While the painting is drying, reread sections of the book that describe the trees, sky, and snow. Point out the phrases that are similes. Using these as models, work with students to create other similes.

   Write "The tree stood as still as _____" on the chalkboard. Have students copy and complete this simile, or have students write a complete simile of their own. Glue the similes to the bottom or back of their paintings.

John Schoenherr • Owl Moon

Note: Reproduce this page onto an overhead transparency to use with "Draw an Owl" on page 75.

Draw an Owl

How to Draw an Owl

1.

2.

3.

4.

John Schoenherr • Owl Moon

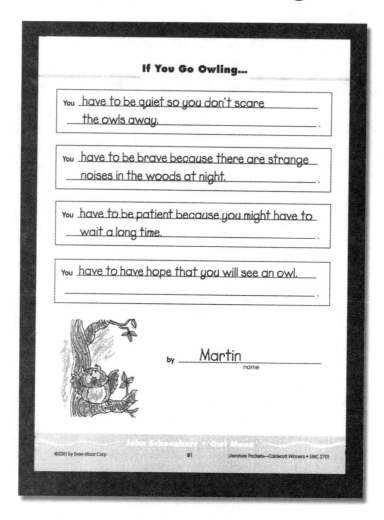

Students recall events and then make charts of "owling" advice.

Materials

- 9″ x 12″ (23 x 30.5 cm) colored construction paper
- page 81, reproduced for each student
- scissors
- glue
- pencil
- crayons

Steps to Follow

1. Reread the book to find the things you need to do if you go owling (you have to be quiet, you have to make your own heat, etc.). List these on the chalkboard.

2. Using the form on page 81, students make a chart of "owling" instructions.

3. Glue the completed list to a sheet of construction paper.

John Schoenherr • Owl Moon

If You Go Owling...

You _____

_____ .

You _____

_____ .

You _____

_____ .

You _____

_____ .

by _____

name

Literature Pockets—Caldecott Winners • EMC 2701

Leo and Diane Dillon

Why Mosquitoes Buzz in People's Ears

About Leo and Diane Dillon......................**pages 83 and 84**
Share the biography of Leo and Diane Dillon and make their bookmark.

Pesky Mosquito Stick Puppet......................**pages 85 and 86**
This little mosquito is perfect for buzzing around students' friends to tell secrets or stories.

African Animals ....**page 87**
In *Why Mosquitoes Buzz in People's Ears*, the animals are outlined in white with spaces in between filled with bold colors. Students create a jungle of wonderful animals in a similar style.

Animal Poems.....................**pages 88 and 89**
Students follow a simple pattern to create lovely poems about their jungle animals. Post the poems on a bulletin board along with their animals for everyone to enjoy. When the pictures and poems come down, place them in students' Dillon pockets.

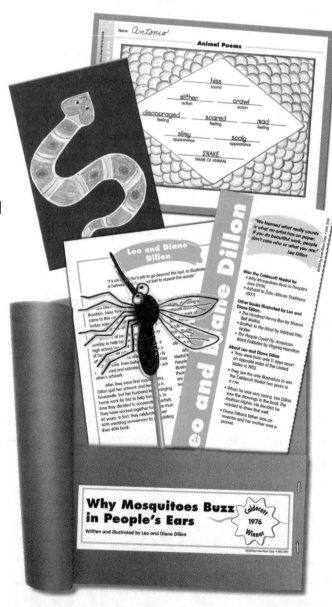

Leo and Diane Dillon

"It's an illustrator's job to go beyond the text, to illustrate what is between the lines, not just to repeat the words."

Leo Dillon was born March 2, 1933, in Brooklyn, New York, to black parents who came to this country from Trinidad. Diane Sorber was born March 13, 1933, to white parents near Los Angeles in California.

A friend of Leo's father came every Sunday to help Leo with his art. After high school Leo went to Parsons School of Design. After a few art classes at two other colleges, Diane also came to study art at Parsons. Even before they met, they had noticed and admired a piece of each other's artwork.

After they were first married, Mrs. Dillon quit her artwork and became a housewife, but her husband kept bringing home work for her to help him with. In time they decided to cooperate as artists. They have worked together for more than 40 years. In fact, they celebrated their 40th wedding anniversary by completing their 40th book.

The Dillons work together gathering ideas, choosing a style, and passing the artwork back and forth as they work. When a work of art is finished, they can't tell who did what. They like to use all kinds of materials and techniques. They have illustrated many kinds of books and have also worked on covers for record albums and magazines.

After winning their first Caldecott Medal for *Why Mosquitoes Buzz in People's Ears*, the Dillons wrote and illustrated *Ashanti to Zulu* which won them their second Caldecott. So far they are the only artists to win the Caldecott two years in a row.

The Dillons live in New York City. They have one son, Lee, who is a painter, sculptor, and jewelry craftsman.

Leo and Diane Dillon

"We learned what really counts is what an artist has on paper. If you do beautiful work, people don't care who or what you are."

Leo Dillon

Won the Caldecott Medal for
- *Why Mosquitoes Buzz in People's Ears* (1976)
- *Ashanti to Zulu: African Traditions* (1977)

Other books illustrated by Leo and Diane Dillon:
- *The Hundred Penny Box* by Sharon Bell Mathis
- *Brother to the Wind* by Mildred Pitts Walter
- *The People Could Fly: American Black Folktales* by Virginia Hamilton

About Leo and Diane Dillon
- They were born only 11 days apart on opposite sides of the United States in 1933.
- They are the only illustrators to win the Caldecott Medal two years in a row.
- When he was very young, Leo Dillon saw the drawings in the book *The Arabian Nights*. He decided he wanted to draw that well.
- Diane Dillon's father was an inventor and her mother was a pianist.

Caldecott 1976 Winner

Why Mosquitoes Buzz in People's Ears

Written and illustrated by Leo and Diane Dillon

Pesky Mosquito Stick Puppet

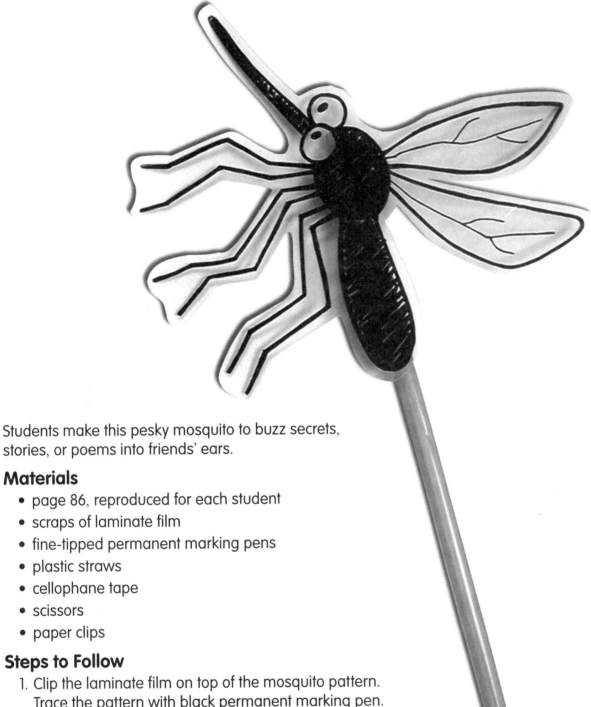

Students make this pesky mosquito to buzz secrets, stories, or poems into friends' ears.

Materials

- page 86, reproduced for each student
- scraps of laminate film
- fine-tipped permanent marking pens
- plastic straws
- cellophane tape
- scissors
- paper clips

Steps to Follow

1. Clip the laminate film on top of the mosquito pattern. Trace the pattern with black permanent marking pen. Color in each section of the mosquito OR color the mosquito pattern and then laminate it.

2. Cut out the mosquito and tape it to a plastic straw.

3. Use the mosquito stick puppet to whisper your animal poem (see page 88) in the ear of a friend.

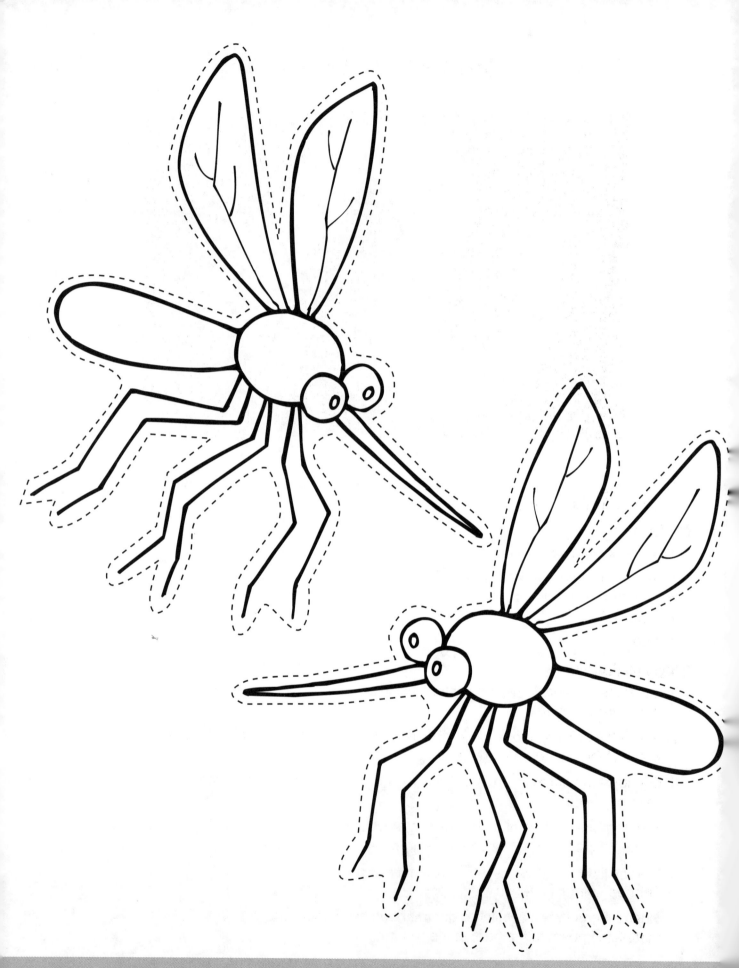

86

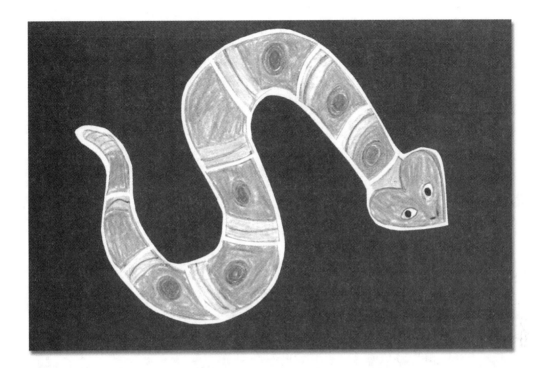

After studying the animals in *Why Mosquitoes Buzz in People's Ears*, have students create their own animals in a similar style.

Materials
- two 9″ x 12″ (23 x 30.5 cm) white construction paper
- 12″ x 18″ (30.5 x 45.5 cm) dark blue construction paper
- crayons or felt marking pens
- scissors
- glue

Steps to Follow
1. Recall the animals found in the story. List these on the chalkboard. Students each select one animal to create.

2. Sketch the animal on one piece of white paper. Using crayons or marking pens, fill in all areas of the animal with bright colors.

3. Cut apart the different parts of the animal's body. The torso may also be cut into several pieces.

4. Reassemble the animal on the second piece of white paper. Lay out the animal, leaving a narrow white space in between each piece. Glue the pieces in place.

5. Cut around the outside of the whole body, leaving a narrow band of white. Glue the finished animal to the dark blue paper.

   Extend the activity by writing a poem about the animal (see page 88). Glue the completed poem to the back of the picture.

Animal Poems

Each animal in *Why Mosquitoes Buzz in People's Ears* has a different story to tell and a different sound associated with its movements. Review the illustrations to find all of the animals, including the minor characters that have little or no role in the text. Create a class poem working together, or have each student select one animal and create a poem about it.

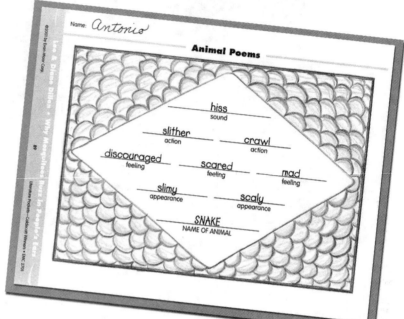

Materials
- page 89, reproduced for each student
- crayons
- pencils

Steps to Follow

Class poem:

1. Write the following headings on the chalkboard: sound, action, feeling, appearance.

2. Select an animal from the story.

3. Review the pages with text and pictures of that animal. Find or create words that fit under each heading. Write these words under the appropriate heading on the board.

4. Select the best words from the chalkboard for the poem. Agree as a class on what words to use for each part of the poem. Write these on the board following this pattern:

sound

action   action

feeling   feeling   feeling

appearance   appearance

NAME OF ANIMAL

5. Students copy the poem onto the form (see page 89) and then add a colorful border to make a frame for the poem.

Individual poems:

1. Select an animal from the story. Review the pages with text and pictures of that animal. Find or create words that describe the animal's sound, action, feeling, and appearance. Write these words on lined paper. (These are notes for the final poem.)

2. Select the best words for the poem. Fill in the spaces on the poem form.

3. Add a colorful border to make a frame for the poem.

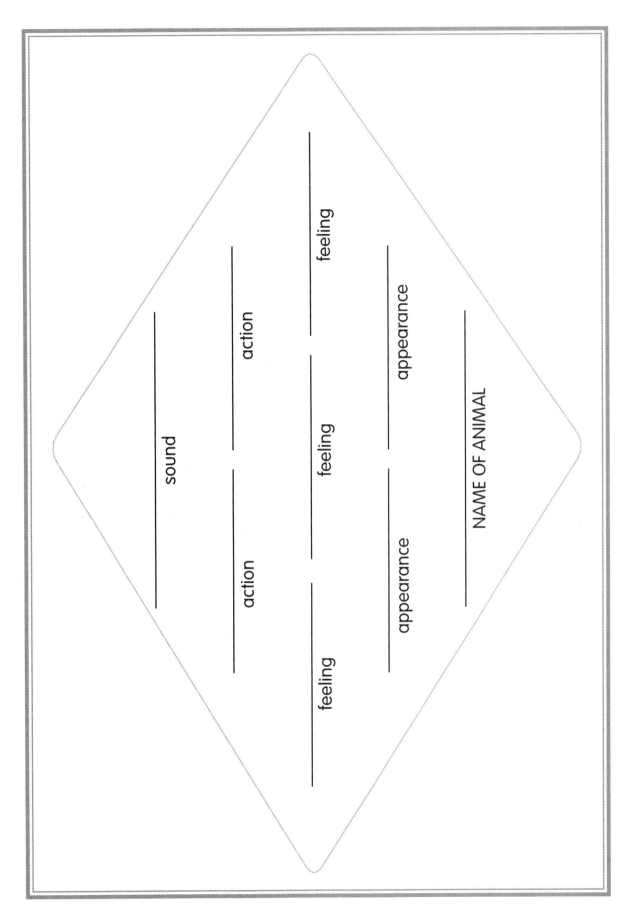

feeling

sound

action

action

feeling

feeling

appearance

appearance

NAME OF ANIMAL

Gerald McDermott

Arrow to the Sun: A Pueblo Indian Tale

About Gerald McDermott ... pages 91 and 92
Share the biography of Gerald McDermott and make his bookmark.

Arrow to the Sun .... page 93
Make an overhead transparency of page 93. Students work together to fill in the chart describing how the colors, shapes, and lines are used to illustrate *Arrow to the Sun*. Students may make a copy of the chart if desired.

Sun and Arrow .... pages 94 and 95
Students make a folder with a colorful "sun" that shines brightly against the dark sky. Outside, an arrow carrying a message soars upward.

Being Brave.................................. page 96
Ask students to recall what the boy in the story did to prove he was brave. Students then write about a time in their own lives when they were brave *(didn't cry when getting a shot; sang a solo in church; caught a high ball even though afraid of it; went into class at a new school all by myself; etc.).*

Gerald McDermott

"The childhood discovery that I could make my 'imaginings' into pictures set me firmly on the path of the artist."

Gerald McDermott was born January 31, 1941, in Detroit, Michigan. He began going to art lessons when he was 4 years old. He says he has had a brush in his hand ever since. After high school he went to the Pratt Institute of Design in New York.

Gerald's first artistic work was an animated film. He began making short films while still in high school. His first film, *The Stonecutter*, required 6,000 frames of art. His career as an illustrator of picture books began when a children's book editor wanted to turn his films into picture books.

The characters in Mr. McDermott's books are brought to life by his dazzling-colored paintings. He often uses patterns and designs of the culture native to the folktale he is retelling. An example is the art in *Raven*, where he used traditional designs from the Pacific Northwest. He often uses no words on pages to let the pictures tell the story.

Mr. McDermott has written three "trickster" tales. The heroes and villains of these folktales—*Zomo the Rabbit, Raven,* and *Coyote*—are often troublemakers. They are also funny and resourceful.

Most of his books were made first as animated films. Then he turned them into books.

Gerald McDermott

> *"One of my greatest joys as a child was to dip a fat brush into a jar of bright paint, to make a glistening sweep across a crisp white sheet of paper."*
>
> *Gerald McDermott*

Won the Caldecott Medal for
- *Arrow to the Sun: A Pueblo Indian Tale* (1975)

Other books by Gerald McDermott:
- *Anansi the Spider: A Tale from the Ashanti* (Honor Book)
- *The Stonecutter*
- *Sun Flight*
- *Daughter of Earth: A Roman Myth*
- *Daniel O'Rourke: An Irish Tale*
- *Raven: A Trickster Tale from the Pacific Northwest* (Honor Book)

About Gerald McDermott
- He was born on January 31, 1941, in Detroit, Michigan.

- From the age of 4, he spent every Saturday in art classes.

- He worked as a child actor for a radio program called *Storyland* until he was 11 years old.

- He worked on *Arrow to the Sun* as a book and a film at the same time.

Caldecott 1975 Winner

Arrow to the Sun: A Pueblo Indian Tale

Written and illustrated by Gerald McDermott

Name:

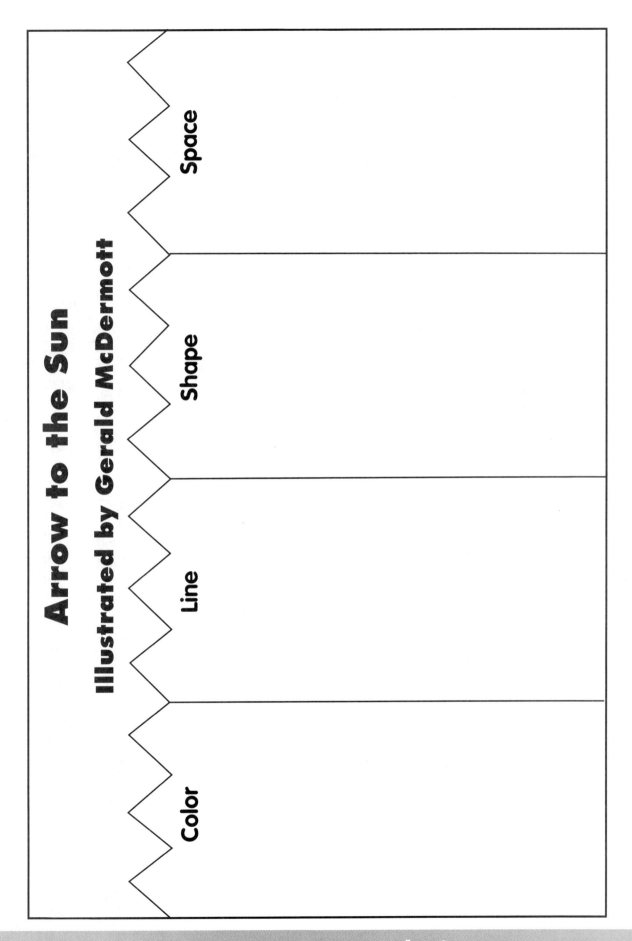

Arrow to the Sun

Illustrated by Gerald McDermott

Color

Line

Shape

Space

Sun and Arrow

Students use shades of orange and yellow to make a spectacular sun and arrow.

Materials

- 12″ x 18″ (30.5 x 45.5 cm) black construction paper
- 6″ (15 cm) square yellow construction paper
- scraps of construction paper in several shades of yellow, orange, and brown
- sun template and arrow form on page 95, reproduced for each student
- crayons—yellow, orange, and brown
- scissors
- glue

Steps to Follow

1. Fold the black construction paper in half to create a folder.

2. Using the circle template on page 95, trace a circle on yellow construction paper. Cut it out and glue it to the inside of the black folder as shown.

3. Using squares, triangles, and rectangles cut from the yellow, orange, and brown construction paper, create a design on the circle to make a magnificent sun. Next, add the sun's rays with the same shapes and colors. The rays should move across the inside of the folder to reach all sides.

4. While the glue dries, cut out the arrow form and complete the sentence.

5. Color the arrow using yellow, orange, and brown crayons.

6. Refold the folder with the sun on the inside. Glue the arrow to the front of the folder.

Gerald McDermott • Arrow to the Sun

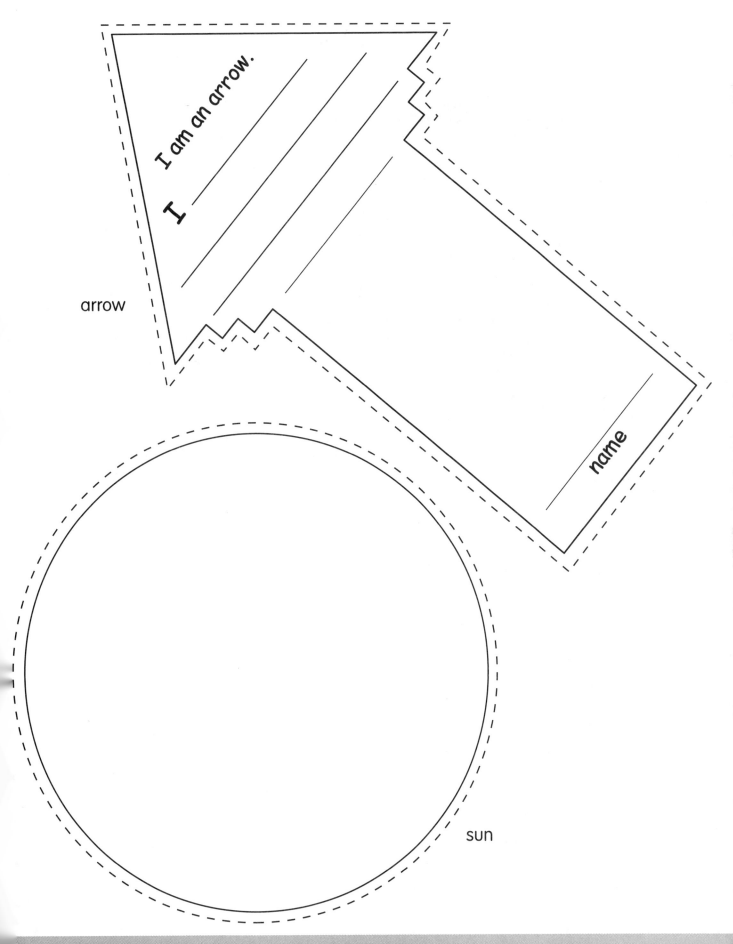

I am an arrow.

I _____

arrow

name

sun

Name: _____

Being Brave

I was brave when _____

_____

_____

_____

_____

_____

_____

_____

Name: _____

Being Brave

I was brave when _____

_____

_____

_____

_____

_____

_____

_____

Gerald McDermott • Arrow to the Sun